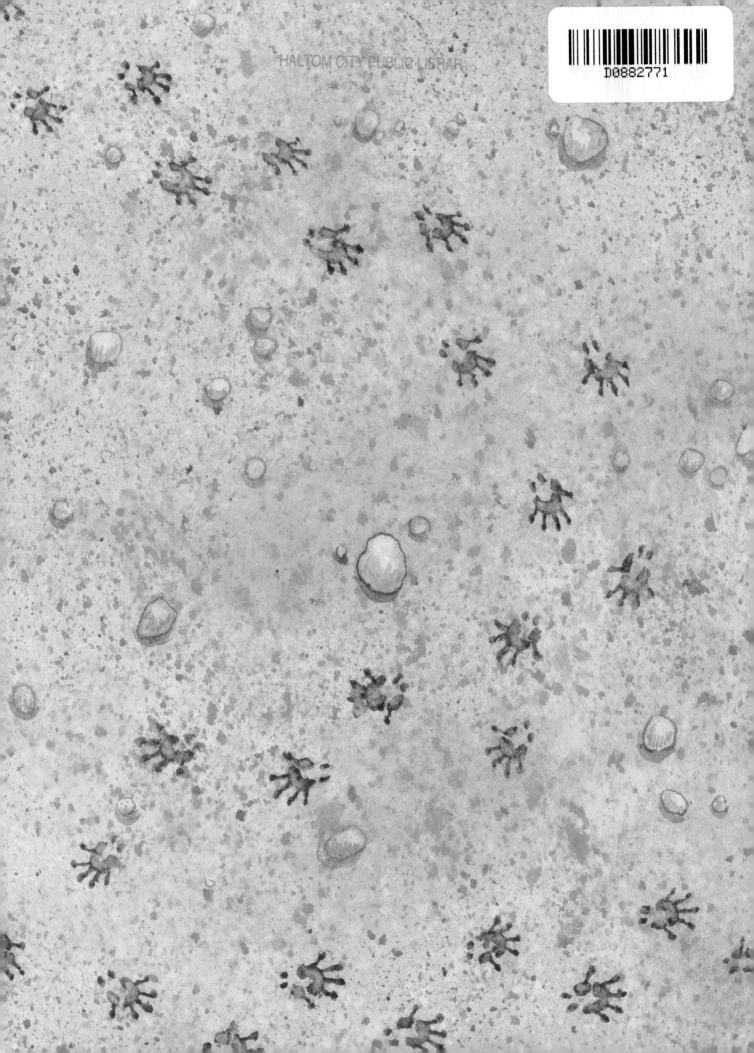

TUESDAY IN ARIZONA

Written by Marian Harris
Illustrated by Jim Harris

PELICAN PUBLISHING COMPANY
Gretna 1998

For Daisy and Piglet

*The word "Pelican" and the depiction of a pelican are trademarks
of Pelican Publishing Company, Inc., and are registered
in the U.S. Patent and Trademark Office.*

Library of Congress Cataloging-in-Publication Data

Harris, Marian, 1961-
    Tuesday in Arizona / by Marian Harris ; illustrated by Jim Harris.
        p. cm.
    Summary: A pack rat causes an old prospector all kinds of trouble,
before brightening up his life.
    ISBN 1-56554-233-9 (hardcover : alk. paper)
    [1. Wood rats—Fiction. 2. Gold mines and mining—Fiction.
3. Arizona—Fiction.] I. Harris, Jim, 1955- ill. II. Title.
PZ7.H24225Tu 1998
[E]—dc21   97-5114
                                                                                    CIP
                                                                                    AC

Printed in Korea

Published by Pelican Publishing Company, Inc.
1101 Monroe Street, Gretna, Louisiana 70053

Before you read this story, you need to know something about pack rats.

This is a pack rat.

You will know that a pack rat lives near you if you see tracks like this close to your house or if you find chewed acorns where you thought you left your toy dinosaur. Pack rats like to collect bright-colored treasures and often drop whatever they happen to be carrying if they find something they think is more interesting.

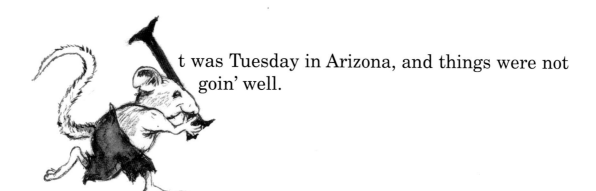 t was Tuesday in Arizona, and things were not goin' well.

But by Wednesday mornin', the banana yucca was blooming and the "trouble" had vanished.

On Thursday it was so hot even the saguaros were droopin'. Only a broad sombrero helped to block the sweltering rays.

But after a little siesta,

somehow, things seemed a little brighter.

Friday, however, ended on a dark and gloomy note. Even a pack rat could see there'd be nothing to nibble in the morning—nothin' but sardines.

But when the sun poked over Hogback Mountain on Saturday,
things were definitely lookin' *up!*

Sunday was a day of rest . . .

'til the neighbors stopped by an' cleaned house.

By the time the sheriff turned in at the lane, all evidence of clutter had been carefully stashed away.

Monday, down at the trading post, all they was swappin'
for pickaxes . . .

was beans.

It was no picnic draggin' them beans 'cross the wrinkles in the road.

But along about the time you could see smoke risin' over the elephant trees, things had eased up considerable.

Monday evenin' things were lookin' mighty bright—

in places like Kansas and Kentucky.

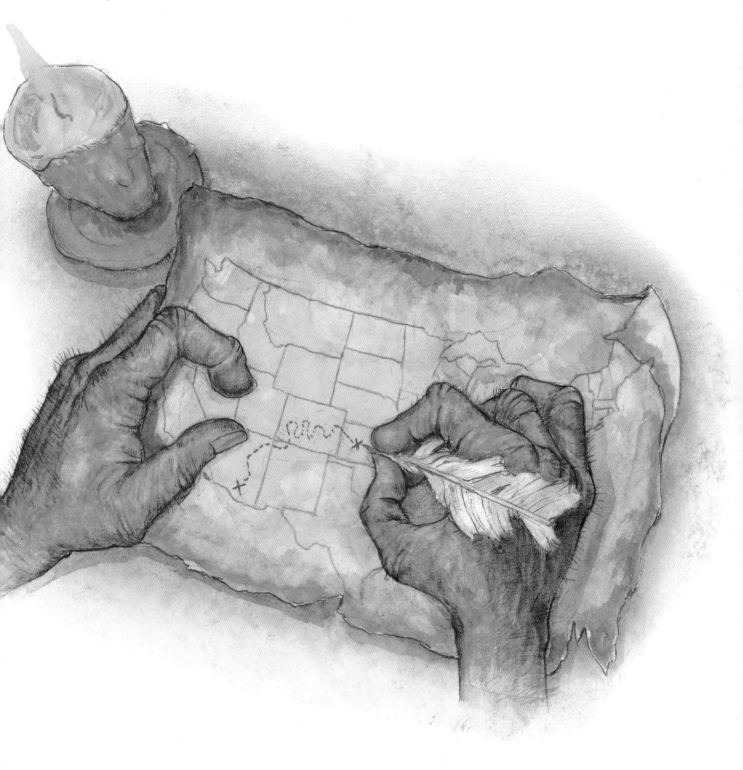

But come midnight, there
was a clinkin' and a rustlin'
down on the sand . . .

and suddenly, prospects close to home was
lookin' brighter than ever!

After all, you jus' never know
what'll turn up next . . .

on Tuesday in Arizona.

THE END